weighted
blankets,
VESTS & SCARVES

Susan White Sullivan

SPRING HOUSE PRESS

Publisher: Paul McGahren

Editorial Director: Matthew Teague

Editor: Kerri Grzybicki

Design: Lindsay Hess

Layout: Ashley Millhouse

Illustration: Carolyn Mosher

Photography: Christen Byrd

Spring House Press

3613 Brush Hill Court

Nashville, TN 37216

ISBN: 978-1-940611-46-4

Printed in the United States of America

First Printing: October 2016

Note: The following list contains names used in *Weighted Blankets, Vests & Scarves* that may be registered with the United States Copyright Office:

Land's End; L.L. Bean; Pellon Wonder-Under; Poly-Pellets by Fairfield; Simplicity; VELCRO Brand Soft & Flexible Sew On fasteners

To learn more about Spring House Press books, or to find a retailer near you, email info@springhousepress.com or visit us at www.springhousepress.com.

contents

about the projects

weighted fabric projects

This collection of weighted garment projects can be helpful for children and adults coping with anxiety, ADD/ADHD, autism spectrum disorder, PTSD, and other sensory disorders. From the weighted bed blanket to the scarf, each offers the comforting presence of deep pressure touch that can make a world of difference for the recipient. The clear and accessible instructions will take you step-by-step through the process while the simple straight-line sewing puts each project within reach of the novice sewist.

bed blanket | 45" x 65"

This snuggly weighted blanket can be customized to any size or weight to suit users of all ages.

14

22

30

vest

I'll guide you through adding interior pockets with weighted pouches to a purchased fleece vest. This easy-to-wear project is great for the classroom or just around town!

lap pad | 9" x 15"

This lap pad is especially useful in school to help the student focus and stay on task. You'll want to make several so you can have one for school, in the car, and at home.

scarf | 5" wide x 30" long, excluding ribbons

This scarf is perfect for on-the-go activities. Adapt the instructions to any size you prefer—longer, wider, or heavier.

26

activity blanket | 40" x 40"

This handy blanket is great for using around the house when the user is enjoying reading, playing games, or watching a favorite movie!

18

a note from the publisher

A weighted blanket changed our life.

Quite a few years ago, our son, Max, was diagnosed with sensory processing disorder, which, as is noted in the introduction, can manifest itself in many different ways. For Max, one of the symptoms was sleeplessness. At bedtime, he would fidget, flip, and flop as he tried to settle himself. When he finally did slumber off, staying asleep was a challenge. So too was trying to function at his best the next day after very little deep sleep. To say that low energy, irritation, and inattention abounded at home due to Max's lack of sleep is an understatement—and that's just the parents I'm talking about. Max had it far worse.

While working with Bernie Hershey, Max's occupational therapist at the Schreiber Pediatric Rehab Center in Lancaster, PA, my wife and I learned about weighted blankets. At the time, there wasn't an easy way to purchase one, but we eventually discovered that a friend's mother, a seamstress, was making them on word-of-mouth referrals. We immediately put in an order for a 6-pound blanket.

Results can vary, but for our family the benefits were instantaneous and transformative. The pressure of the blanket was soothing while the fleece was warm and soft. Max would pull the blanket to his chin, relax, drift off to sleep, and stay asleep. Not only was he getting a good night's rest, but his bedtime routine improved dramatically. After reading, he looked forward to crawling under his blanket because he knew sleep would follow. Max still has the same blanket and, to this day, his bedtime routine is like clockwork—he falls asleep once his head hits the pillow. Best of all, the routine is so ingrained, in the rare instances when he is without his blanket, he can still fall asleep without it.

Sometimes we're asked how we come up with book ideas. In this case, it's a personal reason: we want our DIY and craft audience to know how to make a weighted blanket, scarf, or vest. Whether you're making it for yourself, a family member, or a friend, we love the idea of a craft project capable of calming and comforting a child or an adult. How is that not a good thing?

— Paul McGahren
Publisher,
Spring House Press

introduction

A weighted blanket is exactly what it sounds like—a blanket made heavy by the addition of polypropylene pellets sewn into the blanket itself. More and more, weighted blankets are being used as an effective treatment strategy for children showing the symptoms of sensory processing challenges, including autism spectrum disorders, attention deficit disorders, obsessive compulsive disorders, anxiety, and stress. For those unfamiliar with the sensation of using a weighted blanket, it's comparable to the lead x-ray vest draped on your chest at the dentist's office. In adding physical pressure by applying weight to the body, a weighted blanket—or other weighted garments like a scarf or vest—can help soothe, calm, and regulate children and adults with sensory processing challenges. A weighted blanket is like a warm hug that molds to the body to relax the nervous system.

In the complex nervous system of the human body, the brain receives information through many senses: sight, smell, taste, hearing, movement, balance, and, most relevant to this book, touch. When it comes to touch, we humans are live wires. It has been estimated in the medical community that in one square inch of skin there are: 78 yards of nerves; 19,500 sensory cells at the end of nerve fibers; 160 pressure receptors; 1,300 pain nerve endings; 78 heat sensors; and 13 cold sensors. (Not to mention sweat glands, hair follicles, and blood vessels.) If you extrapolate that one square inch of sensitivity to your entire body, it's easy to understand why not all types of touch are alike and why not everyone responds to touch in the same manner.

When a particular touch nerve ending is stimulated, the nerve transmits the information up the spinal column to the brain, which then interprets that information. Some touch is interpreted as dangerous, and some is interpreted as nonthreatening. In the former instance, the brain sends the direction down the spinal cord to the muscles to move away from the object touching the nerve. An example would be a mosquito landing on your arm. That type of sudden and surprising light touch can be interpreted as a danger to the body. In the latter instance, a deeper, heavier,

and controlled pressure touch is interpreted by most people's brain as calming and nonthreatening. This type of deep pressure touch can be provided by a soothing message, a warm hug, the petting of a dog, or a weighted blanket or garment. As a result, the brain sends a signal to the muscles to move toward the object providing the pressure touch.

This deep pressure touch, as registered by the pressure receptors in the skin and transmitted up the spinal column by the nerves, triggers the release of the famous "feel good" neurochemical serotonin. Serotonin regulates our mood, suppresses pain, calms the body and mind, and reduces anxiety. It ultimately converts to the chemical melatonin, which relaxes the brain and is considered helpful in initiating sleep. And, while the deep pressure touch of weighted blankets, vests, and scarves may not be a remedy for everyone, there are many who have seen positive results immediately in their ability to sleep, sit still, focus, and relax.

Researchers have found that weighted blankets improve sleep in children with attention deficit disorders, autism, and bipolar disorder. A study by N.L. Vandenberg published in *The American Journal of Occupational Therapy* found that wearing weighted garments such as scarves, lap pads, and vests can increase "on task behavior" in children with attention deficit difficulties by "18 to 25%." In 2012, a study published in *Australasian Psychiatry* confirmed "that weighted blankets successfully decreased distress and visible signs of anxiety."

As noted by Angie Rice, Director of Rehabilitation Services at the Schreiber Pediatric Rehab Center, "Being covered with a weighted blanket is just enough deep pressure to help a child feel grounded when out of balance or overstimulated, which in turn leads to success with everyday activities that a child may experience."

The benefits of weighted blankets are not reserved for children: a 2008 Mullen study published in *Occupational Therapy in Mental Health* found that adults who used weighted blankets reported decreased distress and anxiety and improved relaxation.

Research also indicates that the benefits of weighted blankets is extremely varied. In writing *The Weighted Blanket Guide* (Jessica Kingsley Publishers), an excellent primer on the use of weighted blankets, authors Eileen Parker and Cara Koscinski conducted a survey of more than 300 occupational therapists and found that patients using weighted blankets showed improvement not only with autism, attention-deficit/hyperactivity disorder (ADHD), and sensory processing disorder, but with many other conditions, including:

- Post-traumatic stress disorder (PTSD)
- Chronic pain
- Insomnia
- Dementia
- Cerebral palsy

- Chemotherapy
- Mental illness
- Substance/alcohol detoxing
- Restless legs syndrome (RLS)
- Traumatic brain injury (TBI)

Ultimately, weighted garments such as blankets, scarves, and vests are a nonchemical method to help people of all ages. Because they work at a very basic neurological level, these garments do not require any particular level of cognition. They have been safely used over many years with a range of patients from geriatric adults with dementia to small infants.

Because of the many benefits of weighted garments, this new book is timely and necessary. Susan White Sullivan has provided everything you need for making your own weighted blanket, vest, or scarf. Before doing so, however, please work with the guidance of an occupational therapist and use the chart provided so the proper safe levels of weight are used. The clear instructions, crisp illustrations, and helpful photographs will enable patients—or their family and friends—to craft the weighted garments needed to provide the appropriate sensory input that their bodies need to function best.

All of the occupational therapists at Schreiber Pediatric Rehab Center are thrilled to see this book in print and recommend adding a weighted blanket, vest, or scarf to a child's—or an adult's—sensory diet daily!

— **Bernadine Hershey**
Occupational Therapist
Schreiber Pediatric Rehab Center
Lancaster, PA

getting started

All of the projects included in this book are relatively simple. On a scale of 1 to 5, with 5 being the most difficult, none would rate above a 2! All of the sewing is straight lines, except for a few zigzag stitches, and even those could be straight stitches if your sewing machine did not have the zigzag stitch feature. A basic sewing machine will do the job.

What the larger projects do require is patience as you begin adding the pellets. As you progress, the blankets become heavier and a little challenging to handle. You might want to enlist a helper to assist when the blanket becomes heavy enough to be awkward.

A few basic sewing supplies are needed to create the projects in this book.

Before we jump into creating the projects, let's take some time to learn about the special tools and materials you'll need.

Fabrics: I used 100% polyester fleece for the blanket projects, woven cotton for modifying the vest, flannel and cotton for the lap pads, and even a stable soft and stretchy fabric for the scarf. It's really up to you what fabrics you use. They need to be washable, dryable, and woven tightly enough to handle the weight of the pellets. You'll want to consider the climate where the user lives, the season it will be used, and durability. If the item is for a child, it's highly recommended to involve him or her in picking out the fabric once you've decided on the fiber content. They will feel a part of the process and will most certainly feel a connection to their new blanket, vest, lap pad, or scarf.

Pellets: There are a number of products on the market to use in adding weight to your project. After researching what others used and recommended for similar projects, I decided to use Poly-Pellets by Fairfield. I contacted them and they graciously provided Poly-Pellets for the projects. I made a test mini-blanket and was completely satisfied with the results of washing and drying on low temperatures.

Walking foot: I recommend this sewing machine accessory for the bed blanket and activity blanket because you are sewing over a fairly long distance. The walking foot ensures that the top and bottom layers stay aligned, eliminating the chance that either layer ends up longer than the other at the end of the seam. (Quilters use a walking foot to keep the layers of fabric even when they are working on a project.) It's not required; just a suggestion.

Sewing machine needles: A heavy-duty denim needle was used for all projects. The choice is more about the possibility of sewing over pellets and breaking the needle than the weight of the fabric. I used a size 100/16 needle. The 100 is the European number and the 16 is the American number. You may want to have several on hand just in case you experience breakage. Nothing is more frustrating than breaking your last needle when you are just a few seams away from finishing and it's after store hours!

Thread: I used high-quality, 100% polyester thread and matched the thread color to the fabrics. In the case of the blankets and lap pad, the top fabric is a print and the bottom fabric is a solid color. I matched the bobbin thread to the bottom fabric and the top thread to the predominant color in the top fabric.

Marking tools: Water-soluble markers (light and dark) and tailor's chalk are both useful. You may need to experiment to see what works best for you, but you will need some type of marking tool.

Measuring tools: A tape measure and a 12" ruler will help with the scarf, lap pad, and vest. A yard stick is also useful for the blankets.

Straight pins: Good-quality pins that easily penetrate layers of fabric are a joy! Treat yourself!

weight and size recommendations

While doing research for this book, it became clear that there are no hard and fast rules for the size of a weighted blanket or any of the other projects included in this book. There are general guidelines, but ultimately, you will need to decide what works best for your loved one.

When it comes to the topic of weight recommendations, a general consensus can be obtained because there are more sources available for comparison. Note there are no adopted medical standards regarding how heavy a blanket or other weighted item should be, so these are based on my experience and research. Again, you must decide what works best.

weighted sleeping blankets

Weighted blankets intended to be used during sleep have a fairly straightforward formula that appears to be accepted by the weighted blanket community: Calculate 10% of the weight of the user and add 1 to 2 pounds of additional weight. For example, for a child who weighs 45 pounds, the equation would be (45 pounds x .1) + 1 or 2 pounds = 5.5 to 6.5 pounds. For more measurements, see the chart on page 13. For adults, 5 to 10% of ideal body weight is usually recommended.

The sleeping blankets are not intended to hang off the bed, so they typically will not be larger than the mattress's top dimensions, and can be somewhat smaller. The weight that is inserted into the blanket will be distributed over the body of the sleeper. For instance, the bed blanket on page 14 has a finished measurement of 45 by 65 inches. If it is lying flat, it is wider than a twin mattress, but once draped over the user, it wouldn't hang off the bed. The weighted sleeping blanket is intended to be used in conjunction with traditional sheets and blankets.

activity blanket

Our activity blanket is 40 by 40 inches. The weight of this blanket should be decided based on the 10% rule, but do not add the additional 1 to 2 pounds. This blanket is intended to be more portable than the bed blanket.

scarf

The amount of weight for the scarf is typically from 1 to 3 pounds. The dimensions used will greatly affect how much weight can be put into the scarf. The scarf shown on page 26 holds about 16 ounces total. If you prefer a heavier scarf, make it longer and have more pockets to hold additional weight.

lap pad

As with the scarf, the size of the lap pad will play a role in how much weight can be added. Ideally, measure the lap of the user while seated. The finished lap pad should hang down approximately 3 inches on the sides and cover the lap, ending 2 to 3 inches above the knees. Depending on the size of the user, you may be able to enlarge the size and add more weight. The lap pad on page 23 holds 18 ounces.

vest

The great thing about the vest is that you can experiment with the weight by adding more or taking away some of the removable pellet bags. The vest shown on page 31 is a child's size 4/5, and the pellet bags weigh a little over 1 pound total. If your vest is larger, you will possibly have more pockets and more pellet bags.

bed blanket weight recommendations

Body Weight in Pounds	10% in Pounds	Plus 1 Pound	Plus 2 Pounds
20	2	3	4
25	2.5	3.5	4.5
30	3	4	5
35	3.5	4.5	5.5
40	4	5	6
45	4.5	5.5	6.5
50	5	6	7
55	5.5	6.5	7.5
60	6	7	8
65	6.5	7.5	8.5
70	7	8	9
75	7.5	8.5	9.5
80	8	9	10
85	8.5	9.5	10.5
90	9	10	11
95	9.5	10.5	11.5
100	10	11	12
105	10.5	11.5	12.5
110	11	12	13

metric conversions

In this book, I've used inches, yards, ounces, and pounds, showing anything less than one as a fraction. If you want to convert those to metric measurements, please use the following formulas:

Fractions to Decimals

⅛ = .125

¼ = .25

½ = .5

⅝ = .625

¾ = .75

Imperial to Metric Conversion
Length

Multiply inches by 25.4 to get millimeters

Multiply inches by 2.54 to get centimeters

Multiply yards by .9144 to get meters

For example, if you wanted to convert 1⅛ inches to millimeters:

1.125 in. x 25.4 mm = 28.575 mm

And to convert 2½ yards to meters:

2.5 yd. x .9144 m = 2.286 m

Weight

Multiply ounces by 28.35 to get grams

Multiply pounds by .45 to get kilograms

For example, if you wanted to convert 5 ounces to grams:

5 oz. x 28.35 g = 141.75 g

And to convert 2 pounds to kilograms:

2 lb. x .45 kg = .9 kg

bed blanket

Finished size: 45" x 65"

This snuggly weighted blanket can be customized in size and weight to accommodate the needs of all sizes and ages. For children, allowing the recipient to choose fabrics that they love will reinforce their involvement in the process.

materials

- Medium-weight fleece fabric, 100% polyester, 54 to 60 in. wide:
  - Print, blanket front, 2 yd.
  - Solid, blanket backing, 2¼ yd.
- 100% polypropylene pellets
- Thread
- Sewing machine
- Walking foot for sewing machine (optional but helpful)
- Sewing machine needles, jean/denim size 100/16
- Straight pins
- Marking tools: Tailor's chalk or water-soluble marker
- Scissors

BEFORE YOU BEGIN

Weight
Determine the weight, in ounces, of the pellets you will be adding to your blanket. Refer to the chart, page 13, to decide the appropriate total weight to use for your blanket. Divide the number of ounces by 117 (i.e., the total number of squares holding the pellets) to determine the weight in ounces that should be placed in each square.

Pellets
There are a number of pellet products on the market, but Poly-Pellets by Fairfield seem to have received the most favorable recommendations from the weighted blanket community. They are machine-washable and dryable on low heat.

Thread
Different colors of thread were used in the bobbin and top thread to match the fabric. You may want contrasting colors. Use the colors you like best!

Fabric
A medium-weight polyester fleece fabric was used for this project, but there are a multitude of fabrics suitable for this blanket. If your climate is too warm for the fleece, cottons are fine. You will want a washable and dryable fabric with a fairly tight weave that can support the overall weight of the blanket once all the pellets have been inserted. Wash and dry all fabrics before you begin the cutting process to allow for any shrinkage.

instructions

Please read through all of the instructions before you begin.

Note: For all seams, use ½-inch seam allowance. To reinforce stitching to ensure the pellets are captured, backstitch at the beginning and end of each seam.

1. Cut the print fabric for the front to 46 inches wide by 66½ inches long.

2. Cut the solid fabric for the back to 46 inches wide by 72 inches long.

3. Place the two pieces of fabric right sides together and align the sides and bottom. Pin together (see fig. 1).

4. Sew the two pieces together along the sides and bottom. Trim the seam allowances to ¼ inch. Trim corners diagonally (see fig. 2).

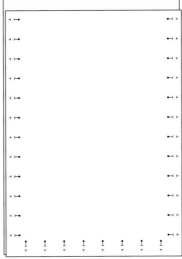

Figure 1

Figure 2

5 Turn right side out. Pin the sides and bottom to flatten the layers. Top-stitch through both layers using a ½-inch seam allowance (see fig. 3).

6 With this step, you are beginning to create the channels in which to pour the pellets. Measure and mark in 5-inch increments across the width of the blanket top. Mark the vertical lines to follow while stitching. You will have eight stitching lines and nine 5-inch-wide channels (see fig. 4).

7 Pinning to ensure the bottom fabric doesn't shift, sew each seam from bottom to top. (It is helpful to begin in the middle and work toward the outside, and to roll up the excess fabric that will need to go through the opening to the right of the needle.)

8 Measure and mark in 5-inch increments vertically, starting from the bottom.

9 Now it's time to start adding the pellets. Using a small measuring cup or whatever works well for you, pour the determined amount of pellets into each of the nine channels. Shake them down to the bottom of the channels.

10 Take the blanket to the sewing machine and sew across the blanket along the marked sewing line closest to the bottom edge of the blanket (see fig. 5). Be sure the pellets do NOT migrate back up to the stitching line. Sewing over the pellets may break the sewing machine needle. It's easier to go slow and be sure the pellets are down in the bottom of the pocket than to attempt to sew over them. Using the heavy denim or jeans needle helps cut down on needle breakage.

11 Continue adding the pellets to each column, shaking them down, and then sewing across the row. The blanket will naturally get heavier with the addition of each row. Just take your time. You may want to enlist a helper to assist you in managing the blanket as it gets heavier. Always position the blanket so that the rows that have had the weight added are to the left of your needle. Figure 6 shows all rows sewn except the top row.

Most weighted blankets are not larger than the top dimensions of the mattress. The blanket is not intended to serve as a regular bed blanket but to be used on top of the regular blanket or sheet.

Approximate Mattress Sizes and Recommended Blanket Measurements

Size	Mattress Dimensions	Blanket Dimensions
Twin	39 x 74-in.	45 x 65-in.
Full	54 x 74-in.	60 x 65-in.
Queen	60 x 80-in.	67 x 70-in.

Figure 3

Figure 4

Figure 5

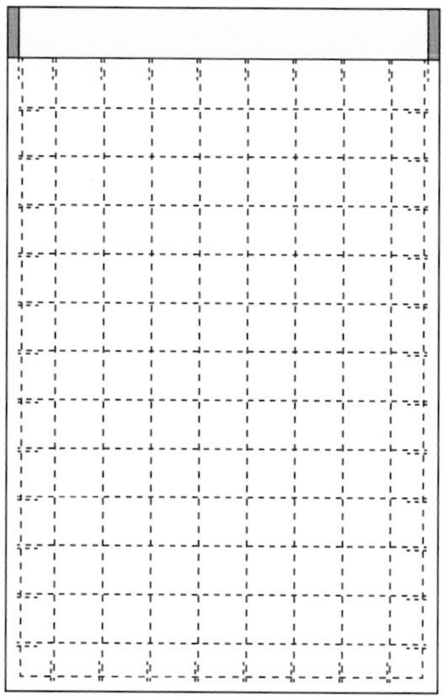

Figure 6

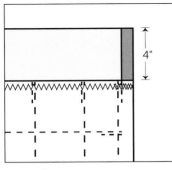

Figure 7

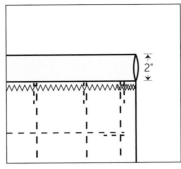

Figure 8

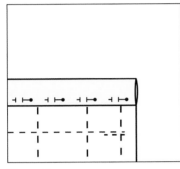

Figure 9

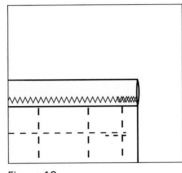

Figure 10

12 When you reach the top of the blanket and are at the top row, add the pellets, shake them down, and pin each pocket in place. It's especially easy to spill the pellets on this last row, so take care to keep the pocket upright as you are sewing. For this last seam, use a zigzag stitch to sew it closed (see fig. 7).

13 Measure and trim the top edge of the backing fabric to 4 inches above the front fabric edge (see fig. 7).

14 Fold the top edge down 2 inches, matching the top edge to the top of the blanket front (see fig. 8).

15 Fold the top edge down onto the blanket front and pin in place (see fig 9).

16 Top-stitch through all layers using a zigzag stitch (see fig. 10).

Congratulations!
Your labor of love is complete and ready to improve the life of your loved one!

activity blanket

Finished Size: 40" x 40"

This smaller blanket is great for those times when concentration is the goal, and it is easier to transport around the house than the bed blanket. Whether the user is reading, playing board games, or drawing and coloring, this blanket may provide a sense of security and calmness that allows the user to fully enjoy the activity.

materials

- Medium-weight fleece fabric, 100% polyester, 54 to 60 in. wide:
  - Print, blanket front, 1¼ yd.
  - Solid, blanket backing, 1⅜ yd.
- 100% polypropylene pellets
- Thread
- Sewing machine
- Walking foot for sewing machine (optional but helpful)
- Sewing machine needles, jean/denim size 100/16
- Straight pins
- Marking tools: Tailor's chalk or water-soluble marker
- Scissors

BEFORE YOU BEGIN

Weight
Determine the weight, in ounces, of the pellets you will be adding to your blanket. Refer to the instructions, page 12, to decide the appropriate total weight to use for your blanket. Divide the number of ounces by 64 (i.e., the total number of squares holding the pellets) to determine the weight in ounces that should be placed in each square.

Pellets
There are a number of pellet products on the market, but Poly-Pellets by Fairfield have received the most favorable recommendations from the weighted blanket community. They are machine-washable and dryable on low heat.

Thread
Different colors of thread were used in the bobbin and top thread to match the fabric. You may want contrasting colors. Use the colors you like best!

Fabric
A medium-weight polyester fleece fabric was used for this project, but there are a multitude of fabrics suitable for this blanket. If your climate is too warm for the fleece, cottons are fine. You will want a washable and dryable fabric with a fairly tight weave that can support the overall weight of the blanket once all the pellets have been inserted. Wash and dry all fabrics before you begin the cutting process to allow for any shrinkage.

instructions

Please read through all of the instructions before you begin.

Note: For all seams, use a ½-inch seam allowance. To reinforce stitching to ensure the pellets are captured, backstitch at the beginning and end of each seam.

1. Cut the fabric for the front to 41 inches wide by 40½ inches long.

2. Cut the fabric for the back to 41 inches wide by 43½ inches long.

3. Place the two pieces of fabric right sides together and align the sides and bottom. Pin together (see fig. 1).

4. Sew the two pieces together along the sides and bottom. Trim seam allowances to ¼-inch. Trim bottom corners diagonally (see fig. 2).

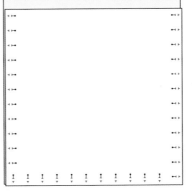

Figure 1

Figure 2

5 Turn right side out. Pin the sides and bottom through both layers to flatten and prepare for topstitching. Top-stitch through both layers using a ½-inch seam allowance (see fig. 3).

6 With this step, you are beginning to create the channels in which to pour the pellets. Measure and mark in 5-inch increments across the width of the blanket top. Mark the vertical lines to follow while stitching. You will have seven stitching lines and eight 5-inch-wide channels (see fig. 4).

7 Pinning to ensure the top and bottom fabrics don't shift, sew each seam from bottom to top. (TIP: Start with the seam on the right side of the blanket and as you move to the left, roll up the excess fabric that will increase as you go.) Remember to backstitch at the beginning and end of the seam.

8 Measure and mark in 5-inch increments horizontally, starting from the bottom.

9 Now it's time to start adding the pellets. Using a small measuring cup or whatever works well for you, pour the determined amount of pellets into each of the nine channels. Shake them down to the bottom of the channels.

10 Sew the blanket along the marked sewing line closest to the bottom edge of the blanket (see fig. 5). Be sure the pellets do NOT migrate back up to the top of the stitching line. Sewing over the pellets may break the sewing machine needle. It's easier to go slow and be sure the pellets are down in the bottom of the pocket than to attempt to sew over them. Using the heavy denim or jeans needle helps cut down on needle breakage.

11 Continue adding the pellets to each channel, shaking them down, and then sewing across the row. The blanket will naturally get heavier with the addition of each row; just take your time. Figure 6 shows the blanket with all seams, except the top row, sewn. (TIP: You may want to enlist a helper to assist you in managing the blanket as it gets heavier. Always position the blanket so that the rows that have had the pellets added are to the left of your needle.)

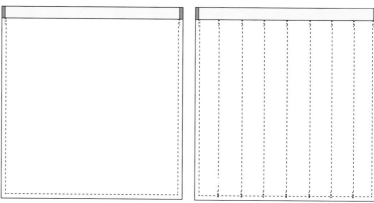

Figure 3   Figure 4

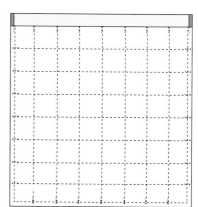

Figure 5   Figure 6

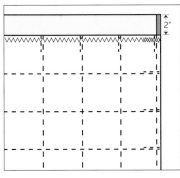

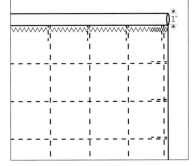

Figure 7

Figure 8

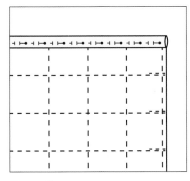

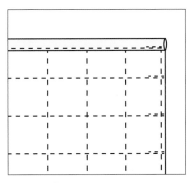

Figure 9

Figure 10

12 When you reach the top of the blanket and are at the top row, add the pellets, shake them down, and pin through both layers at the top of each pocket. It's especially easy to spill the pellets on this last row, so take care to keep the pockets upright as you are sewing. For this last seam, use a zigzag stitch to sew it closed (see fig. 7).

13 Measure and trim the top edge of the backing fabric to 2 inches above the front fabric edge (see fig. 7).

14 Fold the top edge of the backing fabric down 1 inch, matching the top edge to the top of the blanket front (see fig. 8).

15 Fold the top edge down onto the blanket front and pin in place (see fig 9).

16 Top-stitch through all layers to secure them (see fig. 10).

Congratulations!
You've finished making this useful blanket to enhance your loved one's activities around the house.

lap pad

Finished Size: 9" x 15"

Helpful in the classroom, this lap pad can be made just the right size for the user. Again, letting the user choose the fabric lets him or her be involved in the process; or he or she could even help with some of the steps in the construction. You'll end up wanting at least a couple of the pads—one to stay in the classroom, and one for the car. It will especially be appreciated for longer car rides.

materials

- Front, print 45-in.-wide flannel, ½ yd.
- Back, solid 45-in.-wide cotton, ½ yd.
- 100% polypropylene pellets
- Thread
- Sewing machine
- Sewing machine needles, jean/denim size 100/16
- Straight pins
- Marking tools: Tailor's chalk or water-soluble marker
- Scissors

BEFORE YOU BEGIN

Weight
Determine the weight, in ounces, of the pellets you will be adding to the lap pad. See the instructions on page 12. Divide the number of ounces by 15 (i.e., the total number of squares holding the pellets) to determine the weight in ounces that should be placed in each square. Our lap pad contained 1½ pounds, so each square held a little over 1½ ounces of pellets.

Pellets
There are a number of pellet products on the market, but Poly-Pellets by Fairfield have received the most favorable recommendations from the weighted blanket community. They are machine-washable and dryable on low heat.

Fabric
Flannel and cotton were used for this project, but there are other suitable fabrics available, such as medium-weight polyester fleece and corduroy. You will want a washable and dryable fabric with a fairly tight weave that can support the overall weight of the pellets and stand up to everyday wear. Wash and dry all fabrics before you begin the cutting process to allow for any shrinkage.

instructions

Please read through all of the instructions before you begin.

Note: For all seams, use a ½-inch seam allowance. To reinforce stitching to ensure the pellets are captured, backstitch at the beginning and end of each seam.

1 Cut the fabric for the front to 10 inches wide by 16 inches long.

2 Cut fabric for the back to 10 inches wide by 16 inches long.

3 Place the two pieces of fabric right sides together and align the edges. Pin together and sew the two pieces together along the sides and bottom. Trim the seam allowances to ¼-inch. Trim the corners diagonally (see fig. 1).

4 Turn the lap pad right side out. Pin the sides and bottom together to flatten the layers. Top-stitch through both layers along the sides and bottom (see fig. 2).

Figure 1

Figure 2

5 With this step, you are beginning to create the channels in which to pour the pellets. Measure and mark in 3-inch increments across the width of the lap pad top. Mark the vertical lines to follow while stitching. You will have two stitching lines and three 3-inch-wide channels. Pinning to ensure the bottom fabric doesn't shift, sew each seam from bottom to top (see fig. 3).

6 Measure and mark in 3-inch increments horizontally, starting from the bottom. Now it's time to start adding the pellets. Pour the determined amount of pellets into each of the three channels. Shake them down to the bottom of the channels.

7 Sew across the lap pad along the marked sewing line (shown in red) closest to the bottom edge (see fig. 4). Be sure the pellets do NOT migrate back up to the stitching line. Sewing over the pellets may break the sewing machine needle. It's easier to go slow and be sure they are down in the bottom of the pocket than to attempt to sew over them. Using the heavy denim or jeans needle helps cut down on needle breakage.

8 Continue adding the pellets to each row, shaking them down, and then sewing across the row.

9 When you reach the top row of the lap pad, add the pellets, shake them down, and pin each pocket in place. It's especially easy to spill the pellets on this last row, so take care to keep the pockets upright as you are sewing. There should be 1 inch of fabric above the last seam closing the pockets (see fig. 5).

10 Fold the top edge down ½ inch and then ½ inch again. Pin in place and top-stitch through all the layers (see fig. 6). Congratulations! You've completed a travel-size project that will comfort your loved one in the classroom and on car rides.

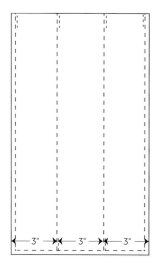

Figure 3

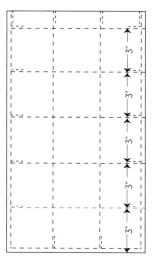

Figure 4

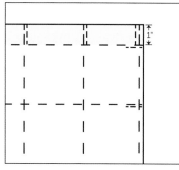

Figure 5

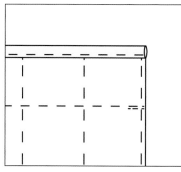

Figure 6

weighted blankets, vests & scarves

scarf

Finished Size: 5" wide x 30" long, excluding ribbons (31½" long, including ribbons)

When an activity is more mobile and makes the lap pad impractical, this scarf may be the solution. Ribbons have been added on the ends for those who would benefit from this type of fidget feature. The pattern is so simple that you can easily make it longer, wider, or heavier. It's all up to you, but these basic instructions will work for any size chosen.

materials

- 57-in.-wide soft nursery fabric, 100% stretchy-but-stable polyester, ⅜ yd.
- 100% polypropylene pellets
- Ribbons, if desired, ¼ yd. each of several textures and widths in colors that coordinate with the fabric
- Thread
- Sewing machine
- Sewing machine needles, jean/denim size 100/16
- Straight pins
- Marking tools: Tailor's chalk or water-soluble marker
- Scissors

BEFORE YOU BEGIN

Weight
Determine the weight, in ounces, of the pellets you will be adding to the scarf. See the recommendations on page 12. Divide the number of ounces by 7 (i.e., the total number of squares holding the pellets) to determine the weight in ounces that should be placed in each pocket. We used 16 ounces (1 pound), and placed approximately 2¼ ounces in each pocket.

Pellets
There are a number of pellet products on the market, but Poly-Pellets by Fairfield have received the most favorable recommendations from the weighted blanket community. They are machine-washable and dryable on low heat.

Fabric
A soft and stretchy, but stable, fabric was used for this scarf, but there are many suitable fabrics. Cottons and medium-weight polyester fleece fabric will work fine. You want a washable and dryable fabric with a fairly tight weave that can support the overall weight of the scarf once all the pellets have been inserted. Wash and dry all fabrics before you begin the cutting process to allow for any shrinkage.

Instructions

Please read through all of the instructions before you begin.

Note: For all seams, use a ½-inch seam allowance, unless otherwise stated. To reinforce stitching to ensure the pellets are captured, backstitch at the beginning and end of each seam.

1   Cut two 6-inch wide by 32-inch long pieces of fabric.

2   If you want to add the fidget ribbons (or just like the look), cut each ribbon into 2-inch lengths. Fold one short end ¼-inch to the wrong side. Fold again ¼-inch to the wrong side and top-stitch through all layers. Alternatively, you could use liquid fray preventative to secure the cut ends. If you choose this method, cut the ribbon into 1½-inch lengths.

3   Align the cut ends of the ribbons with the short edges of one of the fabric pieces (see fig. 1). Be sure to allow for the ½-inch seam allowance on the sides when you pin them in place. Machine-baste the ribbons to the fabric.

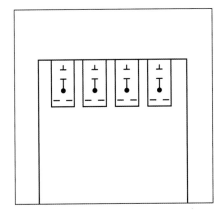

Figure 1

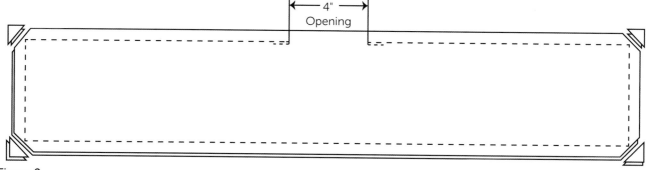

Figure 2

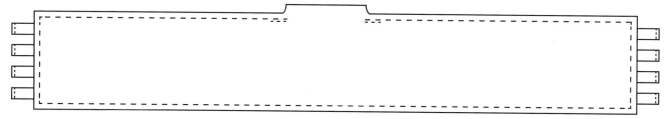

Figure 3

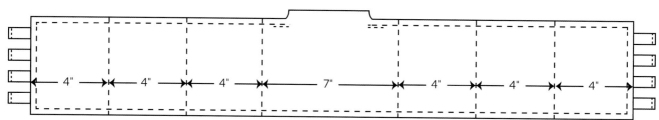

Figure 4

4 Place the two pieces of fabric right sides together and pin together. The ribbons will be on the inside of the fabric pieces.

5 Sew the two pieces together, leaving a 4-inch opening in the center on one long side. Trim the seam allowances to ¼-inch (except at the opening). Trim the corners diagonally (see fig. 2).

6 Turn the scarf right side out. Pin the edges to flatten the layers. Top-stitch through both layers using a ⅛-inch seam allowance (see fig. 3).

7 Measure and mark across the scarf in 4-inch increments beginning at each end. You will have three 4-inch pockets on each end of the scarf and one 7-inch pocket at the center of the scarf (see fig. 4). Do not sew the seams yet.

8 Begin at one end of the scarf and pour in the pellets. Shake them down and sew across the scarf at first marking closest to that end. Add pellets to the second pocket and sew across that seam. Add pellets to the third pocket and sew across that seam. Repeat for the opposite end of the scarf.

9 Add the pellets to the last (i.e., center) pocket. This is the pocket that will sit on the neck; it was intentionally designed to have more space for the same amount of pellets so it is more comfortable on the neck. Shake the pellets down. Tuck the seam allowance into the scarf interior. Top-stitch ⅛-inch through all layers to close the opening.

Congratulations! This on-the-go scarf will give comfort to your loved one wherever they travel.

vest

Using a purchased fleece vest makes creating this project quick and easy. The finished vest is great for sitting in class. The removable pellet bags make laundry day a snap, and also mean you have the option of using the weights or not!

materials

- Purchased vest
- Cotton fabric, 44 to 45-in. wide:
  - Vest lining, ½ yd.
  - Pellet bags, ¼ yd.
- Hook-and-loop sew-on tape (such as VELCRO Brand Soft & Flexible Sew On fasteners), ⅝ x 30-in. package
- 100% polypropylene pellets
- Thread
- Sewing machine
- Sewing machine needles, jean/denim size 100/16
- Straight pins
- Marking tools: Tailor's chalk or water-soluble marker
- Scissors

Weight
Determine the total ounce weight of the pellets you will be adding to your pellet bags, as well as how many bags you will need. The vest shown is a child's size 4 to 5 and has seven pockets in which to insert the pellet bags, so I divided the total number of ounces (18) by seven to determine the weight that should be placed in each pellet bag. If you are making the vest for a larger child or adult, you may need more pockets and more weight, so your math may vary.

Pellets
There are a number of pellet products on the market, but Poly-Pellets by Fairfield have received the most favorable recommendations from the weighted blanket community. They are machine-washable and dryable on low heat.

Thread
Using a color of thread to match the vest will make the seam lines less noticeable. Many of the seams were stitched on top of existing vest seams and are practically invisible.

Fabric
Cotton was used for the interior lining and the pellet bags. I chose a fabric color for the lining that blended with the vest, but had fun choosing something more colorful for the pellet bag fabric since the bags would be hidden. Wash and dry all fabrics before you begin the cutting process to allow for any shrinkage.

instructions

Please read through all of the instructions before you begin.

making & attaching the interior lining

1   Unzip the vest and lay it completely open, wrong side facing up, on your work surface (see fig. 1).

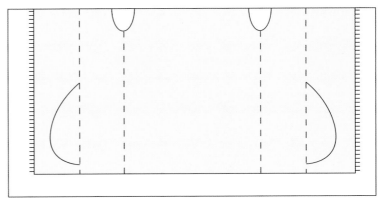

Figure 1

2 To determine the measurement of the fabric piece for the interior lining, measure the width of the open vest and add 1½ inches. For the height, measure the distance from the bottom edge of the vest to the bottom of the armhole. Divide this number by three and add 1 inch (see fig. 2).

3 Cut the fabric to the determined measurements.

4 Hem one long edge (which will be the top of the lining) by folding the top edge ¼-inch to the wrong side and then ¼-inch again. Top-stitch through all layers close to the edge. Repeat for each short edge. Fold and press the bottom long edge ½-inch to the wrong side (see fig. 3).

5 Before you sew the lining to the vest, you will need to determine the placement for the hook-and-loop tape pieces. Place the lining on the open vest with the pressed edge at the bottom and pin it in place. The red dashed lines on figure 4 are the seamlines you will sew along to attach the lining to the vest in step 7. For the vest shown, I divided the length of the lining into seven equal sections and marked these seams on the lining. Cut one 2-inch piece of hook-and-loop tape for each pocket and separate each pair. Center one side of the hook-and-loop tape between the red lines at the top of each pocket indicated by the small black rectangles (see fig. 4), pin it to the lining, and pin the corresponding piece to the vest.

6 Remove the lining and sew the hook-and-loop pieces in place on the lining. For sewing the hook-and-loop pieces to the vest, use matching thread to reduce the visibility and sew each piece separately. (TIP: You can sew one continuous line across the vest over all of the hook-and-loop pieces. I did the latter because it was less distracting visually.)

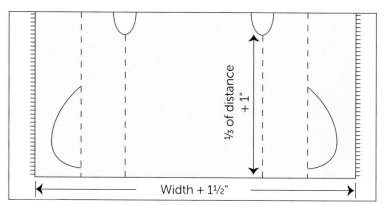

Figure 2

Figure 3

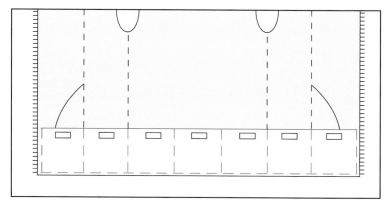

Figure 4

7 Reposition the lining on the vest and pin it in place. Referring to the red dashed lines on figure 4 for placement, sew through all the layers in the following order:

- **Bottom edge:** Sew close to the edge, on top of the existing stitching, if possible.

- **Front edges:** Sew close to the edge of the lining.

- **Side seams:** Sew along the existing side seams.

- **Pocket seams:** Sew along the existing vest pocket seams, if available. If your vest doesn't have pockets, sew the seam an equal distance between the front edge and side seam.

- **Back seams:** Sew along the marked seams.

making the pellet bags

1   For each pellet bag, cut two 5-inch squares of fabric. Placing right sides together, sew around three sides, leaving one side open. Trim seam allowances to ¼-inch and trim the corners diagonally (see fig. 5). Turn the bag right side out.

2   Add the determined amount of pellets to the bag. Tuck the ½-inch seam allowance inside the bag. Shake the pellets to the bottom of the bag and, backstitching at the beginning and end of the seam, top-stitch close to the edge through all layers across the opening (see fig. 6).

3   Insert the pellet bags into the lining pockets and secure the hook-and-loop closures. Congratulations! You've completed a comfortable vest that the user can wear indoors and out.

Figure 5

Figure 6

purchasing or sewing a vest

purchased vests

The vest shown in our photography was purchased from an online retailer. While finding a fleece vest in a local store may depend on the time of year you are looking, you can find them year-round when shopping online. The vest shown in the previous project is made from fleece; most options I found online were also made from fleece, which is best for cool weather or over–air-conditioned buildings.

Here are some great fleece vests from online stores that would be suitable for this project: Land's End #430919 or #430920; L.L. Bean #TA296895 or #TA296896.

The one detail that you will want to be aware of is the shape of the hemline of the vest you purchase. The vest in the previous project had a straight hemline at the bottom edge. Some vests will have a curved hemline. You will need to take that into account when you are measuring and planning the lining piece. You may want to lay a piece of newspaper under the open vest, trace the shape of the bottom edge, and make a pattern for the lining.

purchased sewing patterns

Another option for the experienced sewist is making a vest from a purchased sewing pattern. This will give you much more latitude in the fabric you choose, since fleece may be too warm for some climates. You can apply my instructions for altering a purchased vest to a sewing pattern very easily. As mentioned, the only variation would be if your hemline is a different shape than the vest shown previously, but the modification is relatively easy.

Purchased sewing pattern #1725 from the Simplicity pattern company offers vests sized for the entire family. It is also part of their Learn to Sew line of patterns, ensuring simple construction. Simplicity #8027 is another option.

adding machine appliqué designs

To make your projects even more special, I've included some appliqué designs you can use to add extra personality. Use the alphabet and punctuation to add names, initials, or sayings. There's also an owl, a dinosaur, an open book, and a rocket ship. This feature is intended for use on projects made from cotton fabrics. Once you see how easy it is to use simple shapes to create an appliqué, you just might want to design your own!

supplies

- Fabrics for the backing and for the appliqués: cottons work best
- Paper-backed fusible web (Pellon Wonder-Under was used for the samples shown.)
- Pencil
- Iron
- Sewing machine
- Thread
- Scissors

BEFORE YOU BEGIN

The patterns have several different elements you need to be aware of before you begin.

- The solid black lines are the cutting lines.
- In the case of a design with multiple pieces, the gray shaded areas on the pattern pieces indicate the part of the fabric that will be slid behind another fabric piece.
- The dashed lines on some of the patterns indicate detail stitching that is added after the appliqué pieces have been fused to the project.
- The alphabet letters, numbers, ?, and # will appear backward on the patterns, but once you complete the process, they will read correctly.

The stitching used to sew over the raw edges of the fabric pieces is called appliqué stitch. This is a narrow zigzag stitch with a short stitch length creating a semi-solid line of stitching that makes outlines around the fabric pieces. The goal is sew over the edges, capturing both the top appliqué and the fabric behind it in the zigzag stitch. It secures the raw edges of the fused fabric pieces so they will not fray when washed, but also gives them a nice finished appearance. If you are new to this stitch, practice on some scrap pieces of fabric before you start your actual project.

instructions

Please read through all of the instructions before you begin.

1 Lay the paper-backed fusible web on the pattern, paper side up.

2 Use the pencil to trace the solid black lines of the pattern onto the paper side of the paper-backed fusible web.

3 Cut out the pattern by cutting slightly outside the pattern.

4 Lay the fusible-web side of the pattern onto the wrong side of the fabric piece.

5 Following the manufacturer's directions, use the iron to fuse the pattern piece to your fabric to create the appliqué.

6 Trim the appliqué piece along the pattern lines.

7 Remove the paper from the appliqué piece.

8 Position the appliqué piece on your project, web side down. If the design you are working with has more than one fabric piece, layer the pieces, overlapping as indicated by the shaded areas on the patterns. Determine the order in which to fuse the pieces and start with the bottom piece.

9 Using the iron, follow the manufacturer's directions to fuse the appliqué(s) to your backing fabric.

10 Using appliqué stitch, sew over the raw edges of the fabric pieces and add details as indicated on the patterns by dashed lines.

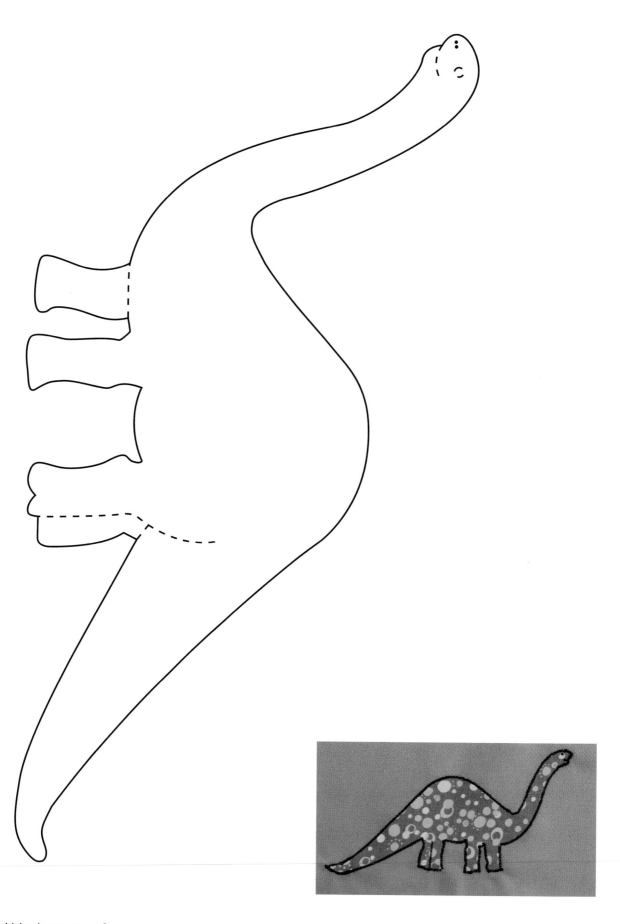

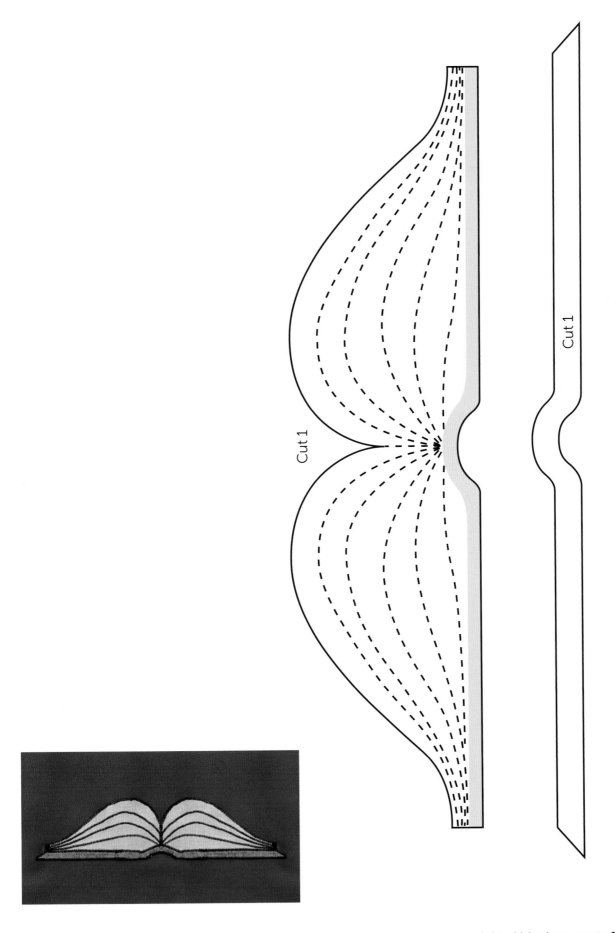

Cut 1

Cut 1

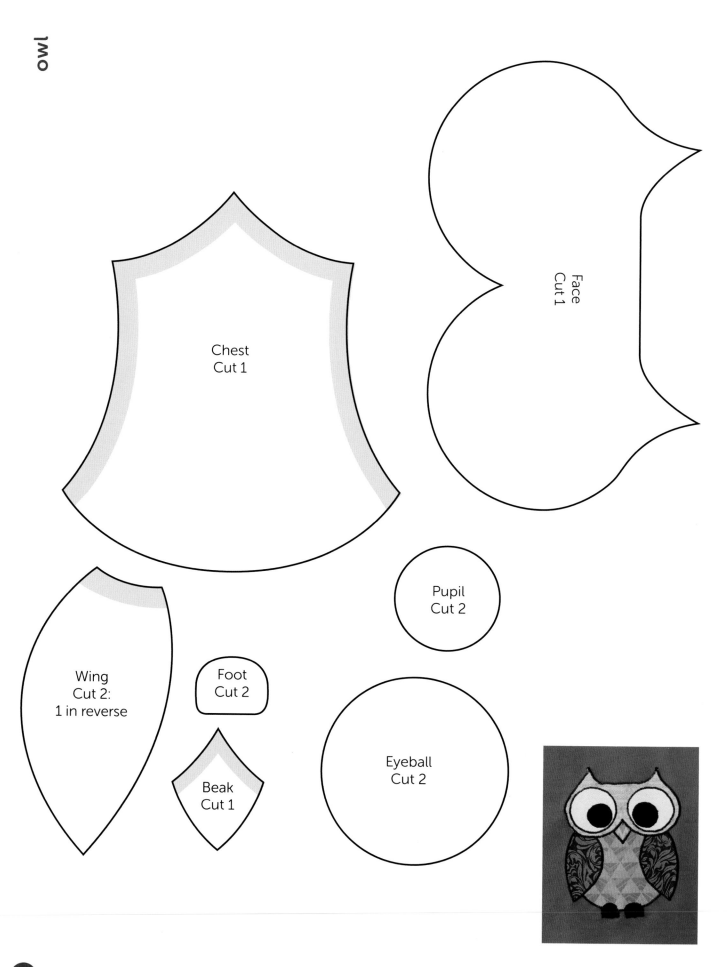

Face
Cut 1

Chest
Cut 1

Pupil
Cut 2

Wing
Cut 2:
1 in reverse

Foot
Cut 2

Eyeball
Cut 2

Beak
Cut 1

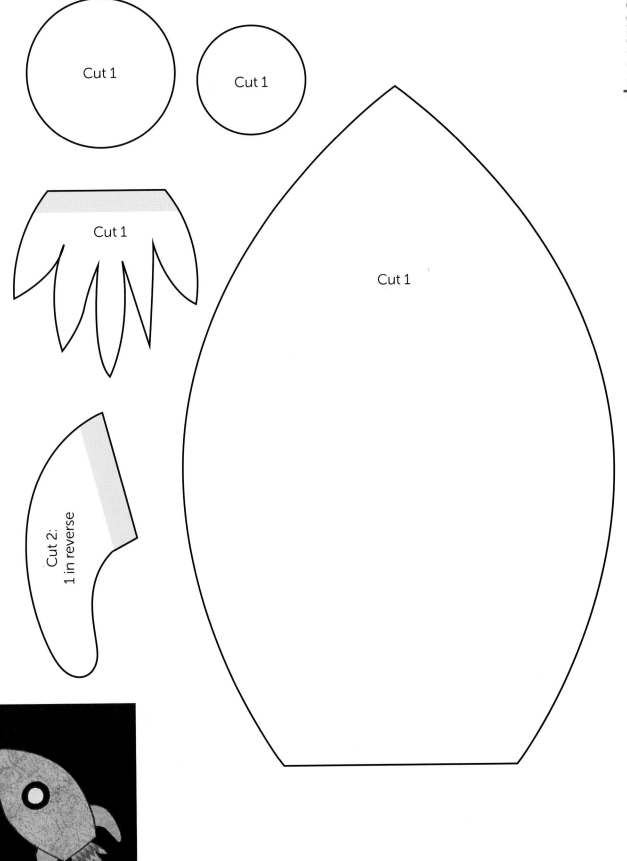

Cut 1

Cut 1

Cut 1

Cut 1

Cut 2:
1 in reverse

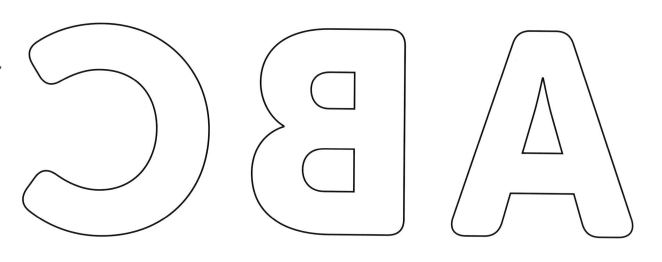

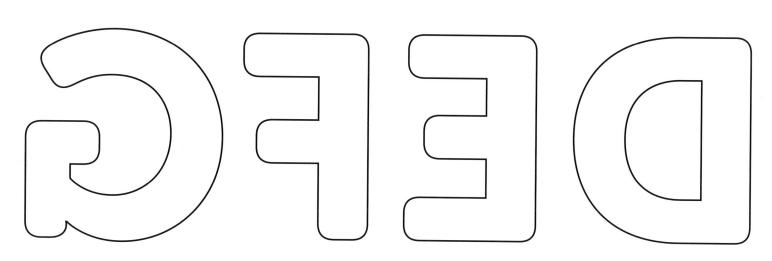

HIJK

LMN

OPQ

R S T

U V W

X Y Z

weighted blankets, vests & scarves

W V U

Σ Y X

+ ? # !

Index

MORE GREAT BOOKS from
SPRING HOUSE PRESS

Fabulous Fat Quarter Aprons
ISBN: 978-1-940611-39-6
List Price: $12.99 | 56 Pages

Fabulous Fabric Jewelry
ISBN: 978-1940611-66-2
List Price: $12.99 | 64 Pages

Christmas Ornaments to Crochet
ISBN: 978-1940611-48-8
List Price: $22.95 | 136 Pages

Crochet Baskets
ISBN: 978-1940611-61-7
List Price: $22.95 | 96 Pages

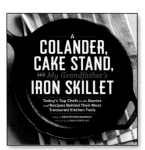

A Colander, Cake Stand, and My Grandfather's Iron Skillet
ISBN: 978-1-940611-36-5
List Price: $24.95 | 184 Pages

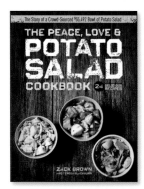

The Peace, Love & Potato Salad Cookbook
ISBN: 978-1-940611-38-9
List Price: $16.95 | 80 Pages

A Natural Beauty Solution
ISBN: 978-1-940611-18-1
List Price: $19.95 | 128 Pages

Peace Work
ISBN: 978-1940611-07-5
List Price: $24.95 | 120 Pages

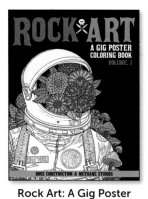

Rock Art: A Gig Poster Coloring Book
ISBN: 978-1940611-42-6
List Price: $12.99 | 80 Pages

SPRING HOUSE PRESS

Look for these Spring House Press titles at your favorite bookstore, specialty retailer, or visit *www.springhousepress.com*.
For more information about Spring House Press, call 717-208-3739 or email us at *info@springhousepress.com*.